YOU CHOOSE BOOKS

D1712702

P9-BAJ-690

EDINBURGH CASTLE

A CHILLING INTERACTIVE ADVENTURE

by Matt Doeden

CAPSTONE PRESS
a capstone imprint

You Choose Books are published by Capstone Press,
1710 Roe Crest Drive, North Mankato, Minnesota 56003
www.mycapstone.com

Library of Congress Cataloging-in-Publication Data
Names: Doeden, Matt, author.
Title: Edinburgh Castle : a chilling interactive adventure / by Matt Doeden.
Description: North Mankato, Minnesota : Capstone Press, [2017] | Series: You
   choose books. You choose: haunted places | Audience: Ages 8–12. |
   Audience: Grades 4 to 6. | Includes bibliographical references and index.
Identifiers: LCCN 2016035558| ISBN 9781515736486 (library binding) | ISBN
   9781515736530 (ebook (pdf)
Subjects: LCSH: Edinburgh Castle (Edinburgh, Scotland)—Juvenile literature.
   | Haunted castles—Scotland—Edinburgh—Juvenile literature. | CYAC:
   Haunted places—Scotland—Edinburgh.
Classification: LCC BF1474 .D64 2017 | DDC 133.1/29413/4—dc23
LC record available at https://lccn.loc.gov/2016035558

Editorial Credits
Mari Bolte, editor; Heidi Thompson, designer; Wanda Winch, media researcher;
Gene Bentdahl, production specialist

Photo Credits
Alamy: Chronicle, 37, Duncan Hale-Sutton, 39, Magnus Pictures, 14, Steven Scott Taylor,
61; © Crown Copyright HES, 57, 94; Dreamstime: Catalina Panait, 25, Chrisdorney,
cover (middle), 1 (middle); Getty Images: Print Collector, 75; Joe Gilhooley Photography,
28, 81; [Mercat Tours IMG_1984] Mercat Tours mercattours.com, 33, [Mercat Tours
IMG_2253] Mercat Tours mercattours.com, 46, [Mercat Tours IMG_2399] Mercat
Tours mercattours.com, 53, [Mercat Tours IMG_2430] Mercat Tours mercattours.
com, 43; Newscom: Danita Delimont Photography/Micah Wright, 21, Design Pics,
88; Shutterstock: Copycat37, 65, Derek Laurence, cover (light), 1 (light), gyn9037,
cover (clouds), happykanppy, background design, Ivica Drusany, 103, jan kranendonk,
79, JoannaTkaczuk, 9, Plateresca, paper design, PlusONE, 70, run4it, ink painting
background, saki80, frame design, Stephen McCluskey, 4, Tamara Kulikova, 6, Tarbell
Studio Photo, cover (tree branch), 1 (tree branch); SuperStock: Jon Arnold Images/Doug
Pearson, 98; Thinkstock: iStock/nonimatge, 84

Printed in Canada.
10050S17

TABLE OF CONTENTS

INTRODUCTION

YOU are visiting the famous Edinburgh Castle, a grand and ancient fortress with a deadly history. As night falls over Scotland, the dark castle looms over the town of Edinburgh. A nighttime adventure quickly turns to terror as the legendary ghosts of Edinburgh begin to stalk you and your friends. Your choices will guide the story. Will you run? Will you hide? Or will you risk everything to delve deeper into the castle in hopes of unlocking its haunted mysteries? Turn the page to find out.

Edinburgh Castle was built on top of Castle Rock in the early 1100s.

INTO THE FORTRESS

"Come on, let's go!" says Keisha, pulling on your arm. You groan. It's been a long day already. You were on the bus before dawn and have since spent hours touring historic Scotland with your class. When you and your friends, Keisha and Mike, hatched your plan to sneak out of your class's hotel and check out Edinburgh Castle at night, the idea had seemed pretty exciting. But now all you want is to go back to sleep.

You look over at Mike. He's always been the reasonable one—cool and calculated, the opposite of impulsive Keisha. But he's also a huge history buff, and he's been preparing for this trip for months. He was crushed when he found out that your brief stay in Edinburgh, Scotland, wouldn't include a tour of the famous fortress.

Turn the page.

The tour guide broke the news early that the castle was closed for renovation and repair, but that didn't make it less disappointing. Mike was feeling down until Keisha suggested you all take a personal tour. "We'll never get another chance to visit a haunted castle—this haunted castle—at night," Mike says with a wink. Unlike Keisha, Mike's a skeptic. He doesn't believe in ghosts.

With a sigh, you pull yourself out of your chair. Tomorrow is the last day of your class trip. Might as well make this last night count. "Okay, let's do it," you say, pulling a sweatshirt over your head and slipping a flashlight into your pocket. And with that, you're out the door of your hotel room and into the cool night air.

You head down the twisted cobblestone streets. Edinburgh is usually a bustling city, yet at this hour it feels almost abandoned.

Castle Rock looms ahead. It's a steep, black, barren rock formation in the center of the city. At the top sits Edinburgh Castle, its outer walls bathed in lights. The three of you pause, looking up at the great fortress. In the distance, lightning flashes, followed by a low rumble of thunder. You feel an impulse to go back. But you know you'll never hear the end of it if you back out now.

Castle Rock stands 250 feet (76.2 meters) above the city of Edinburgh.

Turn the page.

The three of you ascend the rock to the castle grounds. One gate to hop, and just like that, you're in. "Too easy," says Keisha with a mischievous grin.

Another crash of lightning, this time much closer. The thunder follows instantly. You can feel it through the air and through the ground. In an instant, all the lights flicker and die. The castle—this whole part of the city—is engulfed by darkness. Keisha lets out a squeal of delight.

"Now what?" you whisper, trying to keep your voice neutral. Perhaps with the storm and the power outage, Mike will think better of this plan.

No such luck. Mike reaches into his pocket and pulls out a small but powerful flashlight. The beam of his flashlight slices through the darkness before being swallowed up by the volcanic rock.

"I want to see Half Moon Battery," he says. "It was the spot where the castle defenders would fire down on invading armies. Can you imagine fighting for your freedom—and your life?"

Keisha snorts. "We didn't sneak in here to look at rusty old cannons. There's so much other stuff to look at. The vaults! The dungeons! The under-city, where the spirits roam!"

As they argue, you hear something faint in the distance. It's a *rat-tat-tat* noise. Is it a drum? You strain to hear, but the sound is just too soft.

"Well," Keisha blurts out, snapping you out of your trance. "What's it gonna be?"

To go toward the Half Moon Battery, turn to page 12.

To head toward the underground vaults, turn to page 15.

If you're here, you might as well take in some of the sights. And the heart of the castle's defenses sounds a lot more appealing than some grimy dungeon. "Let's check out those cannons," you say, nodding to Mike. He breaks out in a huge grin.

There's something magical and spooky about moving silently through the darkness in this ancient place. All of your senses feel heightened, and there's a strange energy in the air. You can feel your enthusiasm for this adventure growing. Suddenly, you realize that you're glad your friends dragged you out here.

Half Moon Battery doesn't disappoint. It's a massive, curved wall that towers over the city. Even in the darkness of the power outage, the view is stunning—you can see every lantern, candle, or fire for miles.

"Check out these cannons!" Mike shouts.

"Shhh!" Keisha hisses back. In his excitement, Mike keeps forgetting that you're not supposed to be here.

As Mike drones on about how ancient defenders fought off invaders here, you begin to shiver. That energy in the air suddenly feels like it's turned sour. In a heartbeat, your excitement gives way to something else—an unexplained feeling of dread and fear.

You turn to ask if your friends feel it too. But before you can speak, the *rat-a-tat* sound returns. This time, it's not a faint whisper. It's sounds much closer. This time, your friends hear it too.

"Who would be playing a drum out here now?" Keisha asks.

Turn the page.

"Maybe it's some sort of re-enactment of an old battle!" Mike says. "Let's go check it out."

But something about the sound chills you. It doesn't sound like entertainment. It sounds like ... a warning.

To seek out the drummer, turn to page 23.

To suggest getting out of here, turn to page 27.

The cannons displayed in Half Moon Battery today date back to the early 1800s. The battery looks directly over the castle's main entrance.

You have to confess, now that you're here, the spirit of the adventure is growing on you. And what could be better than delving into the depths of a haunted castle? "Sorry Mike," you say with a grin.

The three of you move across the castle grounds as quickly and quietly as you can. The sound of the drums fades, and soon the rumble of thunder and your own footsteps are all you can hear.

"This way," Mike says, leading you on a winding path toward a spot marked Dury's Battery. You manage to find an unlocked gate into the castle, which leads down into the vaults themselves. The vaults, Mike tells you, originated under the 19 arches of South Bridge. Today they make up a huge network of tunnels. They spread out from the castle and run under the city.

Turn the page.

With the power out, your footsteps seem to echo louder than ever. A wet, musty odor hangs in the cool air. You come across a prison cell. Heavy iron bars hang open on rusty hinges.

"There used to be a military prison down here," Mike whispers, shining his flashlight into the pitch-black cell. "I wonder if this is where they kept enemy soldiers?"

Just then, you hear it—footsteps. Loud, clicking boot steps to be precise. And they're headed this way.

"Someone's coming," Keisha says.

To run deeper into the vaults, go to page 17.

To stand your ground and face whoever is approaching, turn to page 19.

To dive into the prison cell to hide, turn to page 49.

"Let's get out of here," you whisper. Mike and Keisha don't need much convincing. The three of you whirl and dart off in the opposite direction. You can feel your heart racing, the sound of your pulse thundering in your ears. Once, you pause to rest. As you try to catch your breath, the sensation of an icy hand reaching out to grab you prickles the hairs on the back of your neck. Still winded, you take off. Charging through the twisting, turning underground vaults, your only care at the moment is escape.

After a minute or two of your mad dash, Mike pulls up. "Wait," he shouts. "Stop."

As the adrenaline rush wears off, you feel suddenly exhausted. Hands on your knees, you bend over, gasping for breath. But then you realize—your trio is now only two.

Turn the page.

"Where's Keisha?" says Mike, shining the beam of his flashlight in every direction.

The two of you shout out for your friend, every call echoing back at you. No answer.

"We have to find her," you say, panic starting to set in. "She could be hurt. Or lost." Mike agrees. But there's one big problem—you're lost too.

"We came from that way," Mike says, pointing. But you're sure that it was the opposite direction.

Mike sighs. "Should we split up?"

The idea of crawling through these vaults alone gives makes your skin crawl. But Keisha's life might depend on you finding her.

To go with Mike, turn to page 42.

To split up and search both directions, turn to page 46.

Every cell in your body is tingling. Adrenaline pumps through your veins as you reach out and grab the hands of your two best friends. Click, click, click. The footsteps are slow and deliberate, but there's no mistaking that they're approaching.

Then, suddenly, they stop. You stand there in complete silence. The beams of your flashlights converge down the passage in the direction of the sound. Ten seconds pass. Twenty.

You let out a breath, only then realizing that you'd been holding it all that time. Keisha and Mike each do the same. Then Keisha starts to laugh. Did you imagine that? Are you all so focused on ghost stories that you conjured up some imagined spirit out of thin air?

Turn the page.

In a moment, all three of you are laughing. You reach out to pat Keisha on the back. But an instant before you do, her eyes grow wide. The potent smell of whisky fills the air. And with a scream, Keisha is thrown straight back into the wall. You gasp as her body slams into the stone. She crumples to the floor, lifeless.

You whirl about, just in time to see the fading figure of a man dressed in high black boots and a tricorn cap. The image lasts only a moment, but it's clear as day. The man is smiling. As Mike rushes to Keisha's side, you find yourself staring at that empty space. A feeling of pure malice hangs in the air.

"Hey!" Mike's call snaps you out of your trance. You join him at Keisha's side. She's sitting now, awake and alert. A thin trail of blood runs down the back of her head.

The castle has served as a home for royalty, a military fort, and a jail for prisoners of war.

"I'm OK," she insists, though her voice quivers. She stands up tentatively. She's a little woozy, but seems otherwise unharmed.

"It was the strangest thing," she says once she catches her breath. "It felt like a wave of pure anger pushing me. I've never felt anything like it. Something didn't want me here."

Turn the page.

"Let's get you out of here," Mike says. "Enough is enough."

"No, no. It's fine," Keisha insists. "Whatever it was, I don't feel it anymore. The spirit is gone now. Let's keep exploring."

To side with Mike and look for a way out, turn to page 30.

To agree with Keisha and delve deeper into the vaults, turn to page 32.

This is too strange not to check out. "I think it's coming from that way," you say, rotating around to point toward the Royal Palace. You can see the jagged outline of the Scottish National War Memorial nearby.

The drumming grows louder. As you move toward the palace, you become more and more dizzy. You stop for a moment. The vertigo is so strong that you fear you might fall over. The sensation is overwhelming. But it passes—at least the worst of it—quickly.

When you stand, everything around you looks blurry. You rub your eyes and shake your head. What's going on?

You turn to look for your friends. But they're nowhere to be found. A mist seems to hang over the place, limiting your visibility in all directions.

Turn the page.

The drumming remains, though. Slowly, almost rhythmically, a figure emerges from the mist. It's a young drummer, the kind once used by armies to relay signals over long distances. The ghostly figure marches slowly as it taps on the drum. Yet you have eyes only for one feature—the only missing feature.

The drummer has no head.

Suddenly, you hear voices behind you, back toward Half Moon Battery. "They're coming!"

There! Another figure. Another. Another! Suddenly, the mist lifts and you find yourself surrounded by people. There are men and boys, of all ages. Or, at least, the faded images of them. But, oddly, these don't seem like ghosts. They seem somehow real ... just insubstantial.

"Fire the cannon!" shouts a voice.

The Scottish National War Memorial was established In the castle In 1927. It commemorates Scottish servicemen and women killed in major wars and campaigns from World War I (1914–1918) through the Gulf War (1991).

"Take cover!" screams another.

You look around. The war memorial has disappeared. You squint in confusion. How could a whole building vanish? A quick glance over the battery reveals a scene that takes your breath away. The castle is under siege. Columns of men march on the fortress, equipped with horses and artillery. Smoke hangs over the invading army. It's as though you've been thrown into the past.

Turn the page.

The soldiers are becoming less and less misty. One nearly solidified figure notices you.

"You there," calls the man. He's short but broad, with a full red beard. "To the walls!"

To rush to the walls to aid in the defense of the castle, turn to page 93.

To ignore the man and take cover instead, turn to page 95.

"Guys, I don't like this," you say. "I think we should head out."

Keisha groans. First you sided with Mike on where to go, and now you're deciding to leave altogether. She's not happy, but Mike agrees with you. "We've had our adventure," he says. "Let's head back."

You leave the castle behind and head out onto the cobbled streets of Edinburgh. Keisha, after a few minutes of sulking, decides that she wants to explore the neighborhood. That seems harmless, so you wander a bit as you make your way back in the direction of your hotel. Even without the blackout, this city has an ancient feel to it. In the darkness, you can imagine what life was like in the 1500s, in the shadow of the castle.

Turn the page.

Keisha can't resist stopping at the famous Greyfriars Kirkyard. With a squeal, she darts into the cemetery. Mike, ever the history buff, isn't far behind. Your only choice is to follow your friends.

If the city feels old, Edinburgh Castle and Greyfriars Kirkyard feel even older. The great stone building of Greyfriars Kirk towers over the graveyard. You're half relieved when you see a sign reading CLOSED. You're not climbing any more gates tonight.

Greyfriars Kirkyard has been used as a burial ground since 1562.

"I wanted to see it," Keisha says, disappointed.

Just then, a frail old man wearing a kilt emerges from the Kirkyard grounds. Where'd he come from? The old man looks like something from out of Scottish history.

"Wanted to see the graveyard, did ye, lass?" he asks Keisha with a wink. "I can open the gate. Just for a quick look."

Keisha looks back over her shoulder, excitement in her eyes. You've already forced her to leave the castle. Do you dare tell her no again?

To accept the old man's invitation, turn to page 36.

To refuse, turn to page 81.

There's no chance you're staying down here a second longer than you have to. "Sorry Keisha. We're outta here."

The way out is a bit more complicated than you'd thought it would be. At every dark corner, you half expect some howling spirit to pop out at you. But nothing does. That sense of menace is gone. Once again, it feels like an empty castle.

Finally, Mike navigates you back above ground and out onto the castle grounds. You inhale the damp night air. Thunder rumbles in the distance, but no rain has fallen yet. Together, you creep forward. The path gently slopes downhill. Walking down and away from the spooky castle is a huge relief.

"Stop," says Keisha, holding up a hand. "Anyone else hear that?"

You start to shake your head when … yes!

"What is that?" Mike whispers. The sound is faint and shrill. It comes in three sharp bursts.

"Look!" Mike points down a pathway. A small figure seems to hover over the ground. It's a dog!

"Come here, fella," Keisha calls. But as the little terrier approaches, you step back. It's definitely a dog—but you can see right through it.

To run from the ghost dog, turn to page 65.

To see what the ghost dog wants, turn to page 69.

You're a bit shaken by what you've seen. But part of you is also thrilled. Now this is an adventure! "I want to keep going," you whisper.

And so, it's deeper into the vaults. The three of you move quickly, but carefully. The vaults were used in the late 1700s by businesses, housing for the poor, and as storage spaces. Now they just look like crumbling tunnels. It seems as though every shelf and doorway could be hiding something sinister.

The air is stagnant and damp. At one point, you notice a distant glowing light ahead. But by the time you reach the spot where you'd seen it, it's gone. You keep moving.

"How long do you think we've been down here?" Mike asks.

The oldest parts of the Edinburgh vaults date back to the 15th century.

It feels like hours. You've gone so far that you know you've left the castle far behind. This network of tunnels branches out beneath Edinburgh. You must be well beneath the city.

"Look at that," Mike says, pointing to a narrow corridor. The passage leads to a room filled with dolls and other toys. As you look over the strange scene, you feel a tug on your shirt.

"Stop it, Keisha," you hiss.

Turn the page.

"What?" Keisha says, from half way across the room. Mike's with her. You whirl around. There's nobody there.

Tug, tug, tug.

"Hey!" you shout, waving your arms all around you.

Behind you, a ghostly figure emerges out of the darkness. It's a little girl clutching a ragged doll. Her hair is messy and hangs over her face. Her arms and hands are thin and gaunt. The figure reaches up toward you, pulling on your shirt. The image lasts only a moment. Then she fades into blackness. Staring at the spot, you rub your eyes, half wondering if you imagined it all.

The look on your friends' faces answers your question before you can ask it. They stare at you, wide-eyed, in disbelief. "Oh no," Keisha moans. "A little girl! That poor, poor little girl!"

"I'll bet people have left these toys for her," Mike says. "Maybe they give the spirit some sort of peace."

"We should leave her something too," Keisha says. But none of you are carrying any toys. "What about a flashlight? Kids love playing with flashlights."

You look down at your hand. The idea of leaving your light down here gives you the shivers. Yet, something about the little ghost breaks your heart. How long has she been here? Is she alone? Despite your reservations, you feel a powerful urge to leave her something.

To leave your flashlight, turn to page 73.

To keep it and move along, turn to page 77.

The look on Keisha's face is so full of hope and excitement. You can't bear to say no to her again. With a sigh, you nod your head. "Just for a minute or two," you say sternly.

"Yeah, yeah. Five minutes," Keisha says. "I promise. Let's go!"

The old man leads you onto the grounds of the graveyard. "The kirk dates back to the 1600s. There are two churches on the grounds," he says. His voice cracks and wavers. It has a strange quality to it. It reminds you a bit of old-fashioned radio broadcasts. "This whole place was a prison once."

"Really?" Mike asks. That's just the sort of thing that would capture his interest. "For enemy soldiers?"

"For the Covenanters," the man replies.

The National Covenant was a written agreement that those who followed the Protestant religion in Scotland would stand firm against persecution. It was signed at Greyfriars in 1638. Those who signed were known as the Covenanters.

"A religious group persecuted by the government," he explains when he sees your confusion. "More than a thousand were locked up here. Terrible conditions. More death and suffering than you can imagine."

"Whoa," Mike whispers.

Turn the page.

"They say the grounds are haunted by the poltergeist of George MacKenzie. They called him Bloody MacKenzie." *His accent makes Bloody sound like Bluidy,* you think. Even after hearing Scottish accents all week, his seems … different.

"Bloody MacKenzie executed hundreds of Covenanters here," the man continues, beckoning. "Come. The tombs are this way."

It's too quiet here, you think. *Too dark. This doesn't feel right.*

The old man leads on. Something about his movement strikes you. It's hard to tell in the dark. But it almost looks like he's not quite walking on the ground. He doesn't disturb a single stone or blade of grass.

A series of stone tombs lies ahead. One is open. It's pitch black inside.

"Can I go inside?" Keisha asks. But there's no answer.

You turn to scan the graveyard. It's just the three of you. The man is gone. But apart from the tombs, the kirkyard is wide open. You would have seen him walk away.

"Sir?" Mike calls out. "SIR?"

"Guess he had to leave," Keisha shrugs. She points to the open tomb. "We're going in."

George MacKenzie's final resting place is known today as the Black Mausoleum.

Turn the page.

"No chance," Mike says, shaking his head. "I've got a thing about small spaces—especially small spaces where they bury dead bodies. As a rule, I don't go inside them."

Keisha turns to you. "C'mon. Don't make me do it alone," she pleads, holding out her hand.

To enter the tomb, go to page 41.

To stay with Mike, turn to page 87.

Taking Keisha's hand, you step inside. The cube-shaped tomb is cold. You can feel the weight of the flat stone ceiling above you. You're not claustrophobic, but the tight space makes you uneasy. The darkness and the hot, stale air makes it worse. Even with your flashlights, you can't see much.

"Where are the coffins?" Keisha asks. She's not the least bit afraid. You can't help but admire her courage.

"I think ..."

A shout interrupts you. It's Mike! Letting go of Keisha's hand, you spin and take a step back toward the tomb's entrance. But then Keisha screams too.

To go to Mike, turn to page 84.

To grab Keisha and pull her out, turn to page 91.

There's no way you're splitting up down here. You've already lost Keisha. Together, you and Mike move through the dark corridors. A long, slow wail echoes through the vault. It's the sound of rusted metal on rusted metal, the slow opening of a long-closed door. The vibration in the air sends chills down your spine.

You come to a series of cells. It looks like all the doors are closed, but upon further inspection, you see the last cell is open. The barred metal door is open just enough to fit a body through. You can make out a faint, pale white light in the back of the cell.

You and Mike exchange a glance. You can see the terror in his eyes—and Mike is not a person easily scared. Your hands are trembling. Your knees feel weak.

Thump … thump … thump.

From 1827 to 1829 serial killers William Burke and William Hare murdered people for cadavers. Rumors say they used the tunnels to move the bodies.

The sound, a low, menacing knock, is coming from within the cell. You creep closer, grabbing onto Mike's arm. You're terrified of what you'll find, but you have to look.

You lean in. What happens next is so fast that you barely process it. A shape rushing out of the cell catches your eye. It's followed by a blinding white light. Then there's a blood-curdling cry that rings in your ears. You scream. Mike echoes you.

Turn the page.

Then the light is gone. All that remains is a high-pitched laugh. Squinting, you look down. Keisha is rolling on the floor, doubled over in laughter. "Oh man, you guys should have seen your faces!" she says, barely able to finish the sentence through her giggling.

For a moment, it takes all of your willpower not to swat her. But then, looking at the stunned expression that's still on Mike's face, you can't help yourself. You start laughing too. Soon, all three of you are chuckling away. The terror of the moment is gone. Suddenly, the fortress is just an old building again.

That's when the ghost appears. It's a woman in a long, flowing dress. Her face shows an expression of terrible pain, as if locked in some soundless scream. She stands there, bound to the wall and unable to move.

"She's burning up!" Keisha cries. Ghostly flames surround the woman as she struggles against her invisible chains. "She needs our help!"

"Are you crazy?" Mike answers, tugging on your arm, pulling you away. "What could we even do? We have to go!"

Could this be the spirit of some poor woman accused of witchcraft? You know they used to burn witches alive. The image fills you with dread; the thought of a ghost witch makes you even more afraid. You can feel your heart almost beating out of your chest.

To try to help the ghost, turn to page 60.

To run, turn to page 64.

The vaults could be crowded places. During the Irish Potato Famine (1845–1847), thousands of Irish immigrants were forced to live in the tunnels.

You hate the thought of splitting up. But you're both so certain that you're right. You've got to give yourselves the best chance to find your friend. You and Mike agree to meet back in the same place in 10 minutes. If you haven't found Keisha by then, you'll get above ground and call for help.

Now that you're alone, the vaults seem somehow darker and colder. Taking slow, careful steps, you creep through the tunnels. You can't help but be fascinated by the stonework, imagining the workers down here building this underground city. The passages seem to hold hundreds of secrets. How far below ground are you? You imagine the weight of the earth pushing down on you. Then you think of the city poor who were forced to call the vaults home. You shudder and fight back a sharp wave of claustrophobia.

Then you hear it—a single, sharp call. Your first thought is that it's Keisha. But no, that wasn't her. That was Mike. You stand in silence, holding your breath.

There it is again! It's distant, but clear. It sounds like, "Help!"

Turn the page.

You turn and dash off in the other direction. Down one corridor, then another. But the cries get no closer, and soon they die out altogether.

The vaults here are smaller, the turns tighter. You must be in an older part of the tunnels. All you can hear now is the huffing of your own breath, the sound of dripping water, and ...

... Bagpipes?

You shake your head, not believing your own ears. But over the past few days in Scotland, you've become very familiar with the eerie, wailing music of bagpipes. And there's no mistaking them now.

To follow the sound, turn to page 52.

To ignore the music and continue your search, turn to page 56.

The *click-clack-click* of a pair of boots draws nearer and nearer. In a panic, Keisha and Mike dart in opposite directions. You click off your flashlight and dive into the dark cell. "Guys!" you whisper as loudly as you can. But they're gone.

What am I supposed to do now?

It's darker than dark here. You can't see a thing. The steps come closer. You slink back into the cell, pressing your back against the cold, rough stone.

A cold breeze wafts down the corridor. You shiver, goosebumps rising up all along your arms. You're almost certain the thunderous thumping of your heart will give you away. It seems you've been holding your breath for minutes.

Turn the page.

The soft glow of a light reflects off the wall outside the cell. It's an odd light—it flickers like a candle, yet something about its color seems almost ... slimy.

The boot steps stop. A pale, ghostlike figure stands outside the cell. Slowly, it turns toward you. As its outline becomes more clear, you see that it's the ghost of a man. It wears high, black boots, a flowing blue cape, and an old-fashioned three-cornered hat. The smell of strong whisky seems to roll off him. Your breath comes in short, panicked bursts. The scent fills your nose and burns your lungs.

The ghost makes eye contact and its face breaks into a slow, terrible grin. You can see the black-as-night gaps where several teeth are missing,

The sound of laughter fills the room, making you cover your ears in pain. But the sound is quickly drowned out by the terrible shriek of rusty metal grinding against itself. *SLAM!* The cell's gate crashes shut.

And just like that, the ghost is gone. Only the echoes of its laughter remain.

You rush to the gate, shaking it with all your strength. The iron won't budge. You shout and shout and shout until your voice is hoarse.

No one is coming. You realize with terror that this cell is not going to be your prison. It's going to be your tomb.

THE END

To follow another path, turn to page 11.
To learn more about Edinburgh, turn to page 99.

Your mind races. Keisha was saying something about the ghost of a piper. You'd sort of tuned her out—she'd been talking about ghosts nonstop since before the trip started.

Something about a secret passage, and a young man sent into the vaults with bagpipes ... You strain to remember more, but you just can't.

The piper—if that really is who you're hearing—seems to be down that corridor. Your flashlight is starting to dim, and you're running out of options. "Here goes nothing," you say, moving toward the sound.

Even under normal circumstances, there's something about the wail of bagpipes that feels a bit eerie. Down here, it's positively spine-chilling. Yet the tune, while slow and mournful, doesn't seem menacing at all.

Edinburgh has been called the most haunted place in all the British Isles.

You trek through the dark passageways, following the music. Once or twice, you think you can spot a faint floating shape ahead. But when you blink, it's gone.

Step by step, you move through the tunnels. When your flashlight finally flickers and dies, plunging you into darkness, your march slows to a crawl. Yet the music seems to keep pace, always distant, but never receding.

Turn the page.

Then, suddenly, there's a light up ahead. You throw an arm over your eyes, which have adjusted to the blackness. In a terrifying confusing instant, you hear the shuffle of footsteps and a shout—your name!

It takes a second to dawn on you. "Keisha!" you shout back. Your friend barrels into you, almost knocking you over, and wraps you up in a bear hug. "Did you hear it too? The bagpipes?" she asks.

You nod, still too overwhelmed to speak.

"I saw him," Keisha whispers somberly. "The piper. He was just a boy. No older than us. Can you imagine it, being alone and lost down here in the dark and cold? How awful that must have been?"

"I ... actually, I can imagine it," you answer with a shudder.

Keisha smiles. "Come on," she says. "He's led us to an exit. He saved us," Keisha says. "I don't know if he can hear me, or understand, but I've asked him to find Mike too."

The two of you climb up out of the vaults. You instantly feel warmer and safer.

You look back. You have a terrible feeling about Mike though. That scream ... then silence. What could have happened? "Hang on, Mike," you call back over your shoulder. "Help is on its way."

You just hope your promise doesn't turn out to be a lie.

THE END

To follow another path, turn to page 11.
To learn more about Edinburgh, turn to page 99.

You close your eyes and take a deep, calming breath. The distant, mournful tune plays on. Strangely, you don't find it frightening. With all you've seen tonight, it seems natural that you should. But all you feel is a wave of sadness.

No time for that, you tell yourself, snapping out of a trance. Your friends are down here, somewhere. You need to find them.

"Mike!" you shout. The syllable echoes off the walls, making your voice sound high and tinny. "Keisha!"

Something pings off a wall. A rock? Something taps your shoulder. You turn, feeling a chill. There's no one there. But someone—or something—definitely laughs.

"Who's there?" you demand.

No answer.

You back away, sweeping the light of your flashlight back and forth. There's definitely no one here.

Unwilling to linger in one place, you move quickly into the ancient vaults. At times, you swear you're being watched. Part of you is searching for your friends. Another part—one you don't care to admit—just wants to find a way out, with or without them.

More than 1.6 million visitors come through Edinburgh Castle every year.

Turn the page.

You come upon a short staircase. You're debating about going up when your flashlight flickers and dies, plunging you into utter blackness. Frantically, you shake the light, hoping to squeeze even a few seconds of life from it. But the batteries are dead.

With a gulp, you start up the stairs. Every step is an unknown. You grope with your feet and hands, searching for each step. One step. Five. Ten.

You reach the top. Your hands run over coarse, rough wood. Could it be a door? You slide your hands down the wood's grain to find a cold, metal handle. You push. You pull. The door won't budge. You bang on it and shout. "Is there anyone there? Anyone! Help me!"

You sense movement at the bottom of the stairs. A white, hazy figure stares back at you. There's no way to escape. Your heart races as panic sets in. You hurl you body against the door with all your might. Nothing happens.

You throw yourself on it even harder, but accidentally hit your head. Disoriented, you turn to charge again, but you lose your balance. You feel the hard impact of the first half-dozen stairs. But you're out cold before you reach the bottom. Unconscious, you're spared the image of the cold, white figure approaching. It comes closer, closer, closer, until ...

THE END

To follow another path, turn to page 11.
To learn more about Edinburgh, turn to page 99.

This has to be the most terrible thing you've ever seen. The idea of being burned alive, the expression of pure agony on the woman's face ... it's all too much to bear. Terrified as you might be, you feel that you have to at least try to help her.

Mike hangs back as you and Keisha step forward. The ghost doesn't seem to even notice you.

"Look," Keisha says, pointing. You look, and notice that there's the faint image of a wooden post. Sections of metal chain bind the ghost to the spot.

You reach out toward the chain, your hand just inches from the writhing figure of the ghost. Although blazing heat is expected, the ghost fire actually feels numbingly cold.

Accused witches were burned at the stake near the castle's Gate House. The Witches Well marks the hundreds of people who were punished for witchcraft in the 1500s.

You wave your hand through one ghost chain. The cold becomes much more intense. But the ghostly chain crumbles and breaks away at your touch. You keep going, breaking each of the chains that bind the ghost. In a moment, she is free.

Turn the page.

The ghost jerks, flying over your heads.
It whirls and spins, meeting you face-to-face.
If she were alive, you'd be able to feel her breath
on your nose. But all you sense is a dull scent of
decay. Her eyes are wild, her expression full of
rage. Suddenly, you feel you may have made the
wrong choice.

"Go!" shouts Keisha. "You're free now!"

For a moment, the spirit hangs there, looking
poised to attack. But then, her expression softens.
The agony in her face fades. In seconds, the wild,
raging ghost is gone.

In her place stands the figure of a young
woman. Her anger is gone—instead, she just
seems sad. The ghost gives you the slightest
nod. A thank you? You can't be sure. Then she
disappears into the darkness, leaving you, Keisha,
and Mike standing in silence.

It's a somber trip back up out of the vaults. None of you speak a word until you're back to the hotel. Long into the night, you toss and turn in your bed. The image of the tortured ghost won't leave your mind. But as terrible as it was, you get a sense of peace when you think about freeing her. Perhaps one day you'll be ready to talk about what happened this night. It would make a great story. Someday.

THE END

To follow another path, turn to page 11.
To learn more about Edinburgh, turn to page 99.

The sight of this writhing ghost makes your heart races and your hands tremble. You want to help, to ease her terrible pain. But you can't bring yourself to take one step closer.

You grab Keisha by the arm and flee the tortured spirit. You have to get out of these vaults, now.

You and Mike seem to be in a similar state of panic. Luckily, Keisha keeps her wits. She leads the three of you all the way to the hotel.

The next day, on the airplane, the shame really hits you. Keisha was strong, but you were not. You wish you could go back and do something—anything—differently. Maybe you could have helped. You'll never know.

THE END

To follow another path, turn to page 11.
To learn more about Edinburgh, turn to page 99.

Enough is enough! You turn and run, but it's too late. The dog barks its cold, ghostly bark, and leaps. You yelp as a freezing sensation grips your leg. It's biting you!

You kick your leg, shouting for help. Mike tries to swat the apparition away. But his hand passes right through the dog's body. Panic growing, you let out a scream.

The first pet burials in the Soldier's Dog Cemetery date back to the 1840s.

Turn the page.

It's over in an instant. As soon as Mike shines his flashlight at the dog, it disappears into thin air. You fall to the ground, clutching your leg. The chill running through the entire limb has you shivering.

Keisha helps you roll up your pants. The mark is clear as day. It's the shape of a dog bite. But the skin isn't broken. Instead, each tooth mark is a frosty blue.

"Hey there!" A deep, bellowing voice shouts from the distance. The beam of a powerful flashlight sweeps across the three of you, locking on.

Two security guards approach. They begin to scold you for being here, when one of them notices your leg.

"He's bit," Keisha says meekly. "By . . . something. It's hard to explain."

"Aye," says one of the guards in a heavy Scottish accent. "I see you've met our ghastly guard dog."

You don't know how to respond. Your jaw hangs open.

"Don't worry," says the man, stroking a scratchy-looking beard. "It won't kill ye. The mark will fade before dawn."

"This has happened before?" Mike asks, dumbfounded.

"Aye," he says nodding. His scowl has been replaced with a grin. "Not in some time, though. He only bites the ones who are marked."

Turn the page.

You finally find your voice. *"Marked?"*

The man nods. "Wouldn't come here at night again, if I were you. Some people just seem to draw out the ghosts of the castle. Nobody knows why. But if the worst you get is a ghostly dog bite, you should count yourself lucky and get along."

You're not about to argue. You can hear the guards making light jokes about ghost dogs and scared tourists as the three of you leave. Sullen, you head for your hotel.

Marked by the spirit world? You're not sure you like the sound of that. You feel very eager to leave Scotland behind you.

THE END

To follow another path, turn to page 11.
To learn more about Edinburgh, turn to page 99.

After any number of apparitions seen tonight, a ghostly dog just doesn't seem that scary. You can't help but wonder why the spirit of an animal would be tied to this place. You take a step toward the apparition.

"Whoa, what are you doing?" Mike asks, grabbing your arm.

"I just want to see what it wants," you answer, taking another step.

The small white figure backs up a step. Then another. The grounds are silent, but you can almost imagine the little guy growling at you.

You follow the figure down a path, coming to a plaque that stands before a small, walled-in garden. The plaque reads: DOG CEMETERY.

Turn the page.

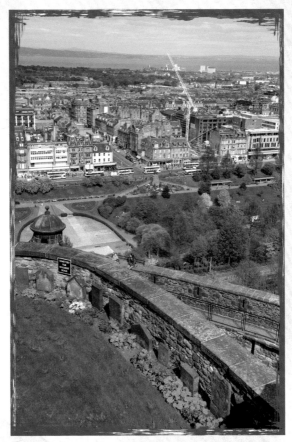
Soldier's dogs and army regimental mascots are buried in the pet cemetery.

"Oh no," Keisha says. "This is way too much for me."

"Yeah, let's get out of here," Mike agrees. "The next creepiest thing to people ghosts is their pets."

But something draws you to this place. You hop up onto the short stone wall that surrounds the small patch of grass. Small tombstones, each decorated with patches of flowers, line the cemetery. As your feet hit the ground on the other side, you hear the sudden sound of barking. Not one dog, but dozens.

You spin around to look at your friends to tell them everything is OK, but you can't see anything. It's as if a wall of fog has fallen over the small garden.

Just as you start to panic, the little dog appears again. Only now, it doesn't seem like a ghost. It seems real, and solid. Confused, you kneel down as the dog trots up to you. It rubs its wet nose into your palm. Almost by instinct, you pet the dog's head. It's soft but cold.

Turn the page.

Another dog emerges from the fog. Then another. And another. Big dogs, small dogs, mutts, and purebreds. All of them seem desperate for attention.

You search for a way out. This garden is tiny. Yet no matter how many steps you take, you can't find the wall. Your shouts seem to echo back at you, as though the outside world has vanished.

You're trapped here. And the dogs keep coming. They swarm you and pin you down. They seem to know that you belong to them now.

THE END

To follow another path, turn to page 11.
To learn more about Edinburgh, turn to page 99.

Your gut is telling you to leave something for the spirit of this little girl. You reach out to where she once stood, placing your light on the stone floor. "I'm sorry it's not better," you call out. "It's all I have."

Instantly, the room feels 10 degrees warmer. You linger there a few moments, trying to come to terms with what has just happened. Finally, Keisha takes your arm. "Let's get out of here," she says. "I think that's enough adventure for one night."

Nobody argues. The narrow corridor continues on, and within minutes you emerge onto a narrow street, surrounded on all sides by tall buildings.

Turn the page.

Keisha spots a sign that reads: MARY KING'S CLOSE. "What's that mean?" you ask. Despite having just spent an hour or more in the underground vaults, something about this place makes you feel more claustrophobic than you ever did below ground.

"The street we're on now is called the Royal Mile," Mike explains. "It's the main street in the city. The lanes and alleyways on either side are called 'closes'. Like regular streets, the closes were named for important people. This was one was named after Mary King."

"It's super haunted," he adds, when he sees your glazed-over face. "It was abandoned in 1645 when bubonic plague arrived. Officials sealed the close to prevent the disease from spreading. But lots of people couldn't leave, or decided to stay. More than 300 people were buried alive here. People still call this area the Street of Sorrows."

The plague blazed through the streets of London. In Edinburgh, Mary King's Close was believed to be the last pocket of infected people in the city when it was sealed.

It's a long trek back to your hotel, but you're happy to leave the castle and its sorrowful streets behind. The image of the little girl runs over and over in your mind. None of you say much. You're sure Keisha and Mike are each lost in their thoughts too.

Turn the page.

Part of you feels sadness over all you've seen. But you keep coming back to the feeling in that room when you gave your flashlight to the spirit of a little girl. It was warmth. What does it mean? What was she telling you?

You can't be sure. You'll never be sure. But something about it just feels ... right. You smile as you come within sight of your hotel.

"Here's hoping nobody noticed we were gone," Mike mutters. "Let's get some sleep."

THE END

To follow another path, turn to page 11.
To learn more about Edinburgh, turn to page 99.

You feel a powerful sadness for the spirit of that little girl. And you'd love to offer her a gift. But she's dead, and you're alive, and you might just need that flashlight. There's no way you're giving it up. Not here, in this haunted castle.

With a deep breath, you lead Keisha and Mike down the damp, narrow corridor, following the beam of your flashlight.

"The air feels different here," Keisha says. "And I think I can hear cars. We must be close to an exit."

You like the sound of that. It's been a wild ride, but your nerves have taken about all they can by now. There's no hesitation in your voice when you say, "Let's go then."

Turn the page.

But the vaults of Edinburgh have one last surprise in store. As you quicken your pace, your flashlight flickers and dies. Then Mike's goes out. So does Keisha's. A powerful gust of wind rushes through the corridor, chilling you to the bone.

Something grabs your arm. It's cold, clammy, and strong beyond imagination. You open your mouth to scream, but your lungs suddenly burn in protest. You can't even manage a whimper. The flashlight is ripped from your grasp.

In an instant, it's over. The presence is gone as quickly as it arrived. The only sounds are the deep, rapid, panicked breaths of you and your friends.

"It ... it took my light," says Keisha.

"Mine too," Mike replies.

"We have to go," you whisper. "Move!"

Together, you move through the blackness, hands out in front of you, waving, searching for obstacles. You stumble, trip, and bang your way blindly through the dark. It seems like you'll never be able to escape.

But then, you spot a light ahead. You rush to it, and burst out onto a narrow street lined with tall buildings. "We made it!" Mike shouts. You reach out to hug your friends.

The Castle Esplanade is the flat area in front of the castle's Gate House. It served as a ceremonial parade ground for soldiers.

Turn the page.

That's when you notice the markings on your arm, where the ghostly presence grabbed you. The skin where it touched you is pale white, the mark in the shape of a long, skeletal hand. Keisha and Mike share the same mark. It doesn't hurt. It just feels cold and sort of numb.

You go back to the hotel. You return home. You go back to school. In time, life returns to normal. The mark fades, but it never really disappears. It remains there, forever, as a dark and terrifying reminder of your night in the haunted vaults of Edinburgh.

THE END

To follow another path, turn to page 11.
To learn more about Edinburgh, turn to page 99.

A church has stood on the Greyfriars Kirk grounds since 1620. The current church was built in the early 17th century.

Keisha's look of hopefulness sours as you shake your head. "No thanks, we have to be getting back to our hotel," you explain. "No cemeteries for us. Enough haunted adventures for one day!"

Keisha doesn't say a word, at first. You can tell that she's fuming. As you lead the way back to the hotel, you can feel her staring daggers at the back of your head. Before you reach it, her anger finally boils over.

Turn the page.

"Thanks for a great evening," she hisses.

"Hey, don't blame me. We had to be smart about things."

"Did you even want an adventure at all?" she barks. "It's like you didn't even want to go. We've got one night in the most haunted city on the planet, and you'd rather rot in a hotel room then try to see it. Some friend you are!"

Years later, you think back to that night as the moment when you and Keisha began to grow apart. You and Mike remain best friends, but Keisha slowly drifts away.

That close bond you shared fades—it's as though the shadow of Edinburgh stands between you. You stop hanging out. She sits at a different lunch table and makes a new group of friends.

By the time you graduate, you feel like you barely know her anymore. But you made your choices back at the castle, and you'll have to live with them. Still though—you've lost a friend over some ghosts that were probably never there.

THE END

To follow another path, turn to page 11.
To learn more about Edinburgh, turn to page 99.

Hot and cold spots, odd smells, the sensation of being touched or pushed, odd noises and voices, feelings of discomfort, and ghost sightings have all been reported at the Covenanters Prison.

"Mike!" you shout, rushing out of the opening of the tomb. Your friend lies on the ground, holding his head. His eyes are wide. He looks terrified.

"Something pushed me!" he cries.

SLAM! The sound of the tomb doors banging shut around you sends your heart into your throat.

"Keisha!" You rush to the tomb, desperately trying every door. None of them budge. Faintly, you hear a voice. It's Keisha, and she's calling out for you.

"We have to get help!" Mike says. He's right. There's nothing the two of you can do. You run as fast as you can, out of the graveyard and into the streets. There's no sign of the old man who led you here.

But you're in luck. You find a police officer almost right away. She doesn't believe a word of your story, but she comes with you.

It's more than an hour before they can get the tomb open. You hold your breath, terrified of what they might find.

The tomb is empty. No sign of Keisha. No poltergeist. Nothing.

Turn the page.

Keisha seems to have vanished. The search for her stretches on for weeks. Her face is on the front page of newspapers and websites around the world. No one believes your story of evil spirits. Some even suspect you and Mike of foul play. The police bring you in for questioning over and over again. You can't even go online—the comments about you are too much to bear.

As you sit in the hotel, waiting for Keisha's parents to arrive, you don't know what lies ahead. You're not guilty of anything, except perhaps poor judgment. Yet whether you're officially charged with Keisha's disappearance or not, you know your night in Edinburgh will haunt you for the rest of your life.

THE END

To follow another path, turn to page 11.
To learn more about Edinburgh, turn to page 99.

Part of you doesn't want to let Keisha go into the tomb alone. But a much bigger part wants nothing to do with that dark place of death. Mike's rule seems like a smart one.

"Come on, enough is enough," you say, taking a step back. But Keisha is already walking in without you.

"Shush!" she whisper-shouts from inside the tomb. "Have some respect. This is a graveyard!"

Before you can reply, everything is turned upside down. It happens in a confusing, jumbled flash. Cold hands shove you. Your entire body leaves the ground, and you're pushed away from the tomb. You look up to see a white mist hanging above you. The mist quickly surges toward you, wafting just inches from your face. A sick smell of death and decay overwhelms you. You turn and vomit on the ground.

Turn the page.

As you retch, a loud, terrible *SLAM* shakes the very earth. Weak and still feeling ill, you pick yourself up. The tomb door is closed. Mike is helplessly pulling and pushing on the doors.

"Help me!" Mike shouts. Together, you work on the door. It starts to budge. It feels like someone—or something—is holding it from the other side. The smell of decay returns.

Many blame the spirit of George MacKenzie for hundreds of attacks reported in the cemetery.

"Let her go!" you shout at the door. "Let her go! We're not your enemy! We're not the Covenanters!"

For a split second, the door seems to loosen. The two of you pull with all of your might. "Please let her go!" you shout.

In an instant, the force holding the door is gone. The door flies open. You and Mike rush inside. Keisha is on the floor of the tomb, unconscious. Mike puts a finger to her neck. "She's still alive," he says.

You carry your friend until you can find help outside the cemetery. Keisha is rushed to a hospital. She has no visible injuries. She regains consciousness the next day. But she's changed. Her eyes seem vacant, her gaze permanently locked on something far away. She barely speaks, and won't say a word about what happened.

Turn the page.

Months go by. Then years. You keep waiting. But the old Keisha—reckless, fun-loving, and quick to laugh—never returns. The new Keisha is someone you feel you barely know.

For the rest of your life, you question what happened inside that tomb. What might have gone differently if you'd gone inside with your friend? You'll never get an answer, but it doesn't stop you from wondering.

THE END

To follow another path, turn to page 11.
To learn more about Edinburgh, turn to page 99.

You surge forward into the tomb, grabbing Keisha by the arm.

"I saw something!" Keisha shrieks.

You don't need her to give any more details, because you see it too. *It's the MacKenzie Poltergeist,* you think. Bloody MacKenzie is a swirling cloud of rage trapped in human form. It reeks of death and decay. The spirit floats just above your head, poised to strike. You drag Keisha, who is frozen with fear, out of the tomb. You dive outside yourself moments before the tomb doors slam shut with a thunderous *BOOM!*

Mike is on the ground, holding his head. "Something pushed me," he says, his voice awestruck. "It was like ... like a force of nature. It felt so ... *evil.*"

Turn the page.

"Time for talk later. We have to go. Now!"
You don't get any arguments this time. The
three of you run as fast as you can until you're
off the grounds altogether. The cobbled streets
of Edinburgh carry you back to your hotel. You
pile into the room you and Mike share, huffing
and panting for breath. Keisha and Mike each
collapse onto chairs. Your lungs ache and your
legs are jelly. But there's one more thing you have
to do before you collapse as well.

You reach up and, with a loud *CLICK*, latch
the deadbolt on the door.

THE END

To follow another path, turn to page 11.
To learn more about Edinburgh, turn to page 99.

This can't be real. It has to be a dream. Right? Without giving it much thought, you follow the order, accompanying a group of ghost soldiers to the top of the castle wall. A huge tower—one that you're sure wasn't there before—stands in the middle of Half Moon Battery. You move closer, using its walls for safety.

From this height you can see it all. Red-coated men on horseback charge through the ranks, banners waving. Thick clouds of smoke rise up from British artillery fire. Deep trenches have been dug into the ground around the castle.

Suddenly, a great blast rattles the fortress. A huge chunk of the tower crumbles and crashes down to the ground below. "David's Tower is hit!" shouts a young man.

Turn the page.

an artist's depiction of what David's Tower would have looked like

You lean over the wall for a better view. But, looking down, you don't see the rest of the tower beginning to collapse above you. Pieces of stone tumble down, crashing onto the castle wall. You cry out as the walkway crumbles under your feet.

You're falling. Screaming, flailing your arms, you fall in what seems like slow motion. You hope it's all just a dream. You'll find out soon enough.

THE END

To follow another path, turn to page 11.
To learn more about Edinburgh, turn to page 99.

This can't be real. It has to be some sort of vision. But you're not taking that chance. The drummer's ghost was telling you something, and what he told you wasn't anything good.

You hurry away from the battery. You're just in time—cannon fire slams into a tall tower in the middle of the castle wall. A tower? That wasn't there before! It's real enough now, though. Screams fill the air as the tower buckles and crumbles. You shudder, not wanting to think about how horrible it would be to die that way.

Another blast of cannon fire sends you sprawling face-first to the ground. You crack your head. Once again, the world spins, flickers, and fades away into blackness.

The first thing you hear when you come to is garbled words. There's a hand on your shoulder. It shakes you gently.

Turn the page.

"You there? Hey, you there?"

It's Mike and Keisha. The world—your world—slowly comes back into focus. As your friends help you to your feet, you glance back over your shoulder to the spot where the tower briefly stood. There's no sign it was ever there.

"Where'd you go?" Keisha asks, looking concerned.

"Huh?" you ask.

"You were staring blankly into space," Mike says. "Then, all of a sudden, you turned and screamed. You jumped—it look like you were thrown, but you must have jumped—onto the ground and cracked your head. What was that all about?"

You don't know where to begin. None of it makes any sense.

After a minute of thought, you ask, "Was there a tower there once, long ago?"

"What?" Mike looks confused. "Well, yeah. David's Tower, I think it was called. It got knocked down in some battle with the British, hundreds of years ago. Why?"

You shake your head. "It's nothing. Never mind. I've got a splitting headache. Let's get back to the hotel."

Maybe someday you'll tell them the story. But right now, you just want to get some rest. And maybe pick up a book on the history of Edinburgh Castle ...

THE END

To follow another path, turn to page 11.
To learn more about Edinburgh, turn to page 99.

EPILOGUE:
THE DARK HISTORY OF EDINBURGH CASTLE

Edinburgh, Scotland, is considered by many to be the most haunted city in the world. Believers say that the city's long history of violence, disease, and war has left it filled with restless spirits. The ancient Edinburgh Castle stands at the center of it all. Many believe that some of those who have met a tragic end here linger on as ghosts, haunting the grounds where their lives ended.

Edinburgh Castle stands atop Castle Rock, a slab of jet black volcanic rock that towers 260 feet (80 m) over the city. The high position and steep rock faces made Castle Rock the ideal spot for a fortress, giving occupants miles of clear views and a formidable natural defense.

No one knows exactly when the fortress first appeared. Archaeologists have found evidence of settlements atop Castle Rock that date back to about 900 BC.

Most of the modern structure was built in the midst of a bloody civil war. The Lang Siege from 1571 to 1573 left both the town and castle in ruins. Hundreds of civilians and soldiers were killed. The hundred-foot-tall David's Tower, which had stood since the 1380s, was destroyed. Half Moon Battery was created from what was left of the tower. (The tower's existence would not be rediscovered until 1912.)

The Lang Siege was one of the deadliest in Edinburgh's history, but it was far from the only one. Conflicts in the 1200s and 1300s focused around the fortress. The castle played a pivotal role during the Jacobite Rising of 1745.

Loyalists to the deposed Scottish King James VII clashed with British forces. The Scottish army was able to capture the city of Edinburgh, but never the castle. Eventually they were forced to admit defeat.

Edinburgh's horrors don't end with war. Bubonic plague, also known as the Black Death, swept through the city in 1645. An overcrowded city and large rat population made it easy for the plague to spread. As many as half the city's population met a terrible end. The city was in a panic. In Mary King's Close, the number of infected was especially high. The sick were bricked up in their homes and left to die. Countless more were forced into the city's underground passages to survive or perish.

Some of the city's residents may have remained behind. Today Edinburgh is a hotspot for paranormal activity. Ghost hunters seek out the countless spirits reported in the city and castle.

Perhaps the most famous ghost is the Piper. Legend tells of a bagpipe player sent into Edinburgh's undercity. There, he would walk the vast network of tunnels while people above ground listened and mapped his progress. But it all went terribly wrong when the Piper became lost in the vast tunnels. Yet long after his death—and still to this day—people report hearing the song of the lost Piper.

Some spirits seem harmless. For centuries defenders of the castle reported the ghost of a headless drummer boy. The ghost appears only when the castle is in danger. Another ghost called Jack appears as a young boy. Jack seems only to want to hold the hands of the living. Meanwhile, the spirit of a young girl is said to haunt the under city of Mary King's Close. People bring dolls and other toys to this young spirit. Visitors have even reported the spirit of a ghost dog near the castle's dog cemetery.

Many of these ghosts are harmless. Yet others seem to have darker designs. Among them is Mr. Boots, who takes his name from the high boots he wears. This spirit appears all around the castle, but mainly in the underground vaults. Those who have encountered him report the pungent smell of whisky. Some have said he throws rocks from deep within the vaults. Others claim he tugs on their clothing or whispers warnings.

Throughout its history, the castle has been attacked more than any other in Britain. At least 23 attempts have been made to capture the fortress.

The tales don't stop there. Visitors report ghost sightings of prisoners and soldiers, as well as women burned at the stake, accused of witchcraft. Not far from the castle grounds, at the graveyard called Greyfriars Kirkyard, lurks a presence that seems truly evil. Some believe it is the spirit of George MacKenzie. Nicknamed Bloody MacKenzie, this man executed hundreds of his enemies on the grounds.

Are the ghosts of Edinburgh real? In 2001 a team led by Dr. Richard Wiseman set out to look for proof that the ghosts existed.

The team monitored the castle with high-tech equipment. Meanwhile, they invited volunteers to enter the castle. The volunteers were not given any history of the castle's haunted history. The team sent some people into areas that were reported to be haunted. It sent others into areas where no ghostly activity had been reported.

Each volunteer was asked whether they encountered ghostly activity. Those sent to reportedly haunted areas reported ghosts at a much higher rate than those sent to other areas.

Wiseman's team didn't prove the existence of Edinburgh Castle's ghosts. But their findings did suggest that something is going on there. Could it be that the ghosts are real? Or do some areas simply stoke the imagination more than others?

Perhaps someday, someone will produce proof that the city really is haunted. Until then, some will remain skeptic, while others will believe the ghosts of Edinburgh exist.

TIMELINE

900 BC—The first settlers make their home on Castle Rock.

638 AD—The city is captured by the English and renamed Edinburgh.

c. 1130—St. Margaret's Chapel is built; it is both the oldest building in the castle and the oldest building in Edinburgh.

c. 1139—King David I builds the castle.

1296–1341—Control of the castle changes between English and Scottish rule multiple times.

1356—King David II rebuilds the castle; David's Tower is constructed in the late 1360s.

1562—Mary, Queen of Scots grants land outside the city for use as a cemetery.

1571–1573—English forces attack the city to capture Mary, Queen of Scots. The seige lasts for two years, and becomes known as the Lang Siege. David's Tower is destroyed during the seige in 1573.

1573—Half Moon Battery is built.

1620—The first church is built on Greyfriar's Kirkyard.

1638—The National Covenant is presented and signed at Greyfriar's Kirk.

1639–1640—Covenanters capture Edinburgh Castle twice.

1679—More than 1,200 Covenanters are imprisoned at Greyfriar's Kirkyard.

1688–1746—Jacobite risings take place across Great Britain and Ireland; Scottish troops attempt to take control of the castle several times, but are never successful.

1757—The castle is turned into a prison; prisoners from the French and Indian War (1754–1763), the American Revolution (1775–1783), and the Napoleonic Wars (1803–1815) are kept there.

c. 1840—The first dog is buried at the soldiers' pet cemetery.

1840–1842—A military prison is built at the castle.

1845–1847—The Irish Potato Famine leaves many farmers homeless. One in four people in Ireland emigrate to other countries.

1912—The ruins of David's Tower are discovered during excavations.

1916—Edinburgh is bombed during an attack by German Zeppelin airships.

1927—The Scottish National War Memorial opens.

1995—Edinburgh Castle is named a World Heritage Site by the United Nations Educational, Scientific and Cultural Organization (UNESCO).

GLOSSARY

adrenaline (uh-DREH-nuh-luhn)—a hormone produced by the body in times of stress; adrenaline gives a person a burst of energy

battery (BA-tuh-ree)—a fortified placement for heavy guns or cannon

bubonic plague (boo-BON-ik PLAYG)—a deadly disease that causes high fevers, painful swelling of the lymph glands, and darkening of the skin; during the Middle Ages the plague was quickly spread by fleas that lived on rats

cadaver (kuh-DAH-vuhr)—a dead body that is used for medical or scientific purposes

claustrophobia (KLAH-struh-foe-bee-uh)—the fear of tight spaces

covenant (KUH-vuh-nehnt)—a formal and permament agreement

Covenanters (KUH-vuh-nehnt-urs)—a Christian religious group that was at odds with the Roman Catholic powers in Scotland during the late 1500s and early- to mid-1600s

emigrate (E-muh-grayt)—to leave one's own country to live in another one

famine (FA-muhn)—a serious shortage of food resulting in widespread hunger and death fortress (for-TRUSS)—a building that is well defended against attacks

kirk (KURK)—a church in Scotland or northern England

mausoleum (maw-suh-LEE-uhm)—a large building that holds tombs

paranormal (pair-uh-NOR-muhl)—regarding events outside of what can be explained by traditional science

persecute (pur-suh-KYOOT)—to continually treat in a cruel and unfair way

poltergeist (POLE-tuhr-gyst)—a ghost or other supernatural being that reportedly makes loud noises, moves physical objects, and often has harmful intent

re-enactment (REE-uhn-akt-mehnt)—a performance of an old event, such as a theatrical performance, a battle, or a speech

siege (SEEJ)—a long attack on a well defended fortress or castle

skeptic (SKEP-tik)—a person who questions things that other people believe in

tomb (TOOM)—a grave, room, or building that holds a dead body

vertigo (VUR-tuh-goh))—feeling of dizziness or lightheadedness, often brought on from a fear of heights

OTHER PATHS TO EXPLORE

In this book you've seen how terrifying being alone in a haunted place can be. But haunted places can mean different things to different people. Seeing an experience from many points of view is an important part of understanding it.

Here are a few ideas for other haunted points of view to explore:

* The castle and kirkyard aren't the only haunted places in Edinburgh. Pubs, inns, and theaters also claim to be homes to ghosts. What kinds of ghosts do you think inhabit these areas?

* The legend of the lone bagpipe player in the tunnels is a famous one. Imagine you are the bagpiper. Would you feel afraid in the vaults? What would you do if you were down there, alone? How would you try to escape?

* In the 16th century, dozens of accused witches were tried and tortued before being put to death at the castle. What might it have been like to be accused? Would you be afraid, angry, or both?

READ MORE

Hoena, Blake. *The Tower of London: A Chilling Interactive Adventure.* North Mankato, Minn.: Capstone Press, 2017.

Morey, Allan. *12 Spooky Haunted Places.* Mankato, Minn.: 12-Story Library, 2016.

Owings, Lisa. *Ghosts in Palaces.* Minneapolis: Bellwether Media Inc., 2017.

INTERNET SITES

Use FactHound to find Internet sites related to this book. All of the sites on FactHound have been researched by our staff.

Here's all you do:
Visit *www.facthound.com*
Type in this code: 9781515736486

INDEX